Civil Rights, the Constitution, and the Courts

Civil Rights, the Constitution, and the Courts

ARCHIBALD COX

MARK DeWOLFE HOWE

J. R. WIGGINS

HARVARD UNIVERSITY PRESS

Cambridge, Massachusetts

1967

Contents

Acknowledgment

These papers were originally presented in 1965–1966 as a series of evening lectures at the Massachusetts Historical Society, which has graciously made them available for publication.

Civil Rights, the Constitution, and the Courts

Direct Action, Civil Disobedience, and the Constitution

ARCHIBALD COX

THE PROBLEM OF civil disobedience is as old as Socrates and as modern as Martin Luther King. It presses upon us today because the civil rights revolution suggests, and sometimes seems to legitimatize, new tactics of social and political reform. The movement gathered momentum from the courageous action of individuals asserting simple human rights, usually without violence, in direct challenge to the established order and sometimes in ways that superficially seemed to involve civil disobedience. Reform would not have moved so fast, if it progressed at all, without the freedom rides, the sit-in demonstrations, the Birmingham parades, and the march from Selma to Montgomery. There might have been no Federal equal public accommodations law in 1964 without the sit-ins and demonstrations that brought out "Bull" Connor's police dogs. There might be no Voting Rights Act of 1965 without Selma. Thus a question is raised: If direct action, disobedience of local authorities, and like techniques of the civil rights movement have at last produced a measure of reform in race relations, will they not lead us still closer to the goal in that area and also promote long-overdue reforms in other segments of society? The Supreme Court, the argument runs, has set aside the convictions of sit-in demonstrators in every case to come before it.[1] Should we not infer that other nonviolent disobedience to unjust laws is morally correct and may even be a constitutional right? If we are sensitive to wrongs—war, poverty, and prejudice—why not use the same tactics again to shock the conscience of the people and their elected representatives by riveting attention upon the brutality and injustice that too many of us would like to ignore?

Opposed to this line of thought there is grave concern about what the use of widespread disobedience as a technique of social and political reform is doing for law observance in the United States and indeed to the whole concept of government by law. The question is asked most often by those who oppose all change, including some who did not hesitate to corrupt the processes of law by using them to maintain a caste system and political white supremacy. Others who ask the question, however, have unimpeachable credentials as reformers and defenders of the right of protest. Mr. Justice Black not long ago reminded us "experience demonstrates that it is not a far step from what to me seems the

[1] E.g., Hamm v. City of Rock Hill, 379 U.S. 306; Bell v. Maryland, 378 U.S. 226; Lombard v. Louisiana, 373 U.S. 267; Peterson v. Greenville, 373 U.S. 244; Garner v. Louisiana, 368 U.S. 157.

earnest, honest, patriotic, kind-spirited multitude of today to the fanatical, threatening, lawless mob of tomorrow. And the crowds that press in the streets for noble causes today can be supplanted tomorrow by street mobs pressuring the courts for precisely opposite ends."[2] Burke Marshall, formerly Assistant Attorney General in charge of the Civil Rights Division of the Department of Justice, has written, "I frankly do not know how our society can support, or at least as far as law enforcement is concerned, even tolerate a movement which relies on genuine disobedience to law as its source of energy, and on the threat of violence alone to induce social change."[3]

The two lines of thought are not entirely contradictory, but they do suggest the need to try to clarify as many points as one can concerning the legality and morality of the protest movements.

In the beginning, it is necessary to define much more precisely the different subjects we are talking about. Such simple terms as "direct action," "civil disobedience," and "nonviolent action" are too broad to be useful to a lawyer, and it would seem to me

---

[2] Dissenting opinion in Cox v. Louisiana, 379 U.S. 559, 575, 584.
[3] Marshall, "The Protest Movement and the Law," *Virginia Law Review*, 51 (1965), 785.

that unless defined they must also confuse social and moral judgments. A great deal of mistaken action has arisen from the use of such loose terms as "civil disobedience" to describe several entirely different forms of conduct. Parades are different from sit-ins and sit-ins are different from the deliberate immobilizing of traffic upon city streets. Disobedience of a local statute that violates the Constitution of the United States is altogether different from defiance of a plainly valid law. Let me describe some of the essential differences from the standpoint of their constitutional status before I go on to analyze the moral questions.

The Federal Constitution guarantees extraordinarily wide opportunities to use mass meetings, parades, and similar public demonstrations to express sentiment, dramatize the cause, and demonstrate the aroused indignation, power, and solidarity that secure response from a representative government. The Freedom March held in Washington in the summer of 1963 is a dramatic example. Such demonstrations are within the right of free expression guaranteed against governmental restraint by the First and Fourteenth Amendments, except when they are really force cloaked in the guise of expression as in the case of mass picketing in a labor dispute. They are subject only to those minor regulations of time or place necessary to secure equivalent rights for others.[4]

The prospect that antagonism toward the demonstrators will lead to outbreaks of violence affords no justification for suppressing a demonstration. Constitutional rights may not be denied because of hostility to their assertion. This is not to say that two hostile groups of demonstrators — for example, one group opposing United States' intervention in Vietnam and an opposing group advocating the bombing of Hanoi — must be allowed to march on the same street at the same hour. The Constitution leaves room for such reasonable regulation of the time, place, duration, and manner of demonstrations as may be necessary to prevent private gangs from challenging each other to violence in a manner reminiscent of Hitler's Germany. The State's first duty, however, is to keep the peace by protecting the exercise of constitutional rights — not by suppressing them.[5]

Obviously there can be no legal or moral problem of disobedience if the State or local police authorities permit a demonstration. The ideas expressed, the

[4] The most recent opinions, which collect the precedents, are Edwards v. South Carolina, 372 U.S. 229; Cox v. Louisiana, 379 U.S. 536, Cox v. Louisiana, 379 U.S. 559.

[5] Cox v. Louisiana, 379 U.S. 536, 550-551. But cf. Feiner v. New York, 340 U.S. 315.

grievances displayed, and the solidarity demonstrated are useful, perhaps even necessary, aspects of effective self-government. Whether one joins or not depends upon the extent of his sympathy for the cause and his belief in the value of demonstrations.

The problem arises when the State or local police authorities seek to bar the demonstration. A police chief or sheriff may call it a threat to public order. It may violate a local ordinance. The mayor or other local official may refuse a permit required by local law. Should this occur, as in the South in connection with civil rights demonstrations, three quite different situations may develop.

First, the proposed demonstration may be indisputably an exercise of freedom of speech and liberty to assemble and petition for the redress of grievances. In that event the action of the local authorities would be unconstitutional. Such was the case with most of the civil rights demonstrations. Sometimes the demonstrators who pushed on to exercise their constitutional rights in defiance of local authorities described themselves as engaged in civil disobedience. Their use of the term is highly misleading. One may disregard with legal impunity the commands of civil authorities (but perhaps not of a court[6]) if what the authorities forbid is in truth only

[6] The normal rule is that one who violates an injunction may be punished for contempt of court even though the injunction is vacated

the exercise of a privilege guaranteed by the United States Constitution. Such action involves no civil disobedience—no violation of law in the ultimate sense—because the only orders that are violated are nullities (that is, not law at all) being unconstitutional. To talk about this kind of assertion of constitutional rights as civil disobedience is extremely dangerous because it lumps lawful with lawless conduct and gives the erroneous impression that both are permissible if only one is sympathetic enough to the demonstrators' objectives.

We should put into a second and distinct category the forms of demonstration or individual protest which violate plainly valid and constitutional laws. Sitting down in the White House, in a Selective Service Board office, or in the corridors of the Department of Justice are good examples. There are other places for demonstrations, and no one has a constitutional right to interfere by physical obstruction with the orderly dispatch of public business. The obstruction of the railroad tracks at the Army base in Oakland, California, is another example. No less legally wrong were the occasional actual or threatened civil rights demonstrations deliberately blocking traffic or access to public buildings; they too

---

on appeal. United States v. United Mine Workers, 330 U.S. 258. It is uncertain whether the doctrine applies to injunctions impinging upon freedom of expression.

would violate plainly valid, binding laws. Such tactics are not legally distinguishable from the wrongs committed by Governors Barnett and Wallace when they refused to desegregate State schools in compliance with the final orders of the Federal courts. One can say categorically that there is no constitutional right of civil disobedience to a valid law.

Not one of the great events in the civil rights movement has involved this kind of disobedience to law on the part of the Negroes involved. This was true at Tuscaloosa in 1956, at Little Rock in 1957, during the Freedom Rides in 1961, and at Oxford in 1962. At Selma in 1965 events tottered on the brink. Dr. King made public statements seeming to suggest disobedience of a court order, yet the fact was that in the end he did not disobey but acted on the advice of lawyers in the good faith belief that he was not in contempt of the court.[7]

Between these two categories lies a third made up of cases in which all one can say at the time of the demonstration is that it goes to the outer boundaries of and perhaps exceeds any constitutional right. When there is doubt, the demonstrator takes his chance upon the ultimate decision of the highest court which will hear his case and to which he has the means and perseverance to carry it. If the court

[7] Marshall, "The Protest Movement and the Law," pp. 796-797.

sustains the constitutional claim, he will go free; otherwise he will suffer the penalty. The Constitution does not give anyone a privilege to violate a law in order to test its constitutionality. Recognition of such a privilege would mean that the actual constitutionality of the law could never be tested; the sole issue would be the bona fides of the claim of unconstitutionality.

I do not mean to imply that one who violates a law in a sincere and reasonable but mistaken challenge to its constitutionality should be judged by his fellows or treated by the courts in just the same way as one who violates a decree of the Supreme Court or a law he knows is not subject to serious challenge. All I am saying now is that he is legally guilty and can claim no constitutional protection for his mistake.

Has such a man any better moral claim? Is there ever a social or moral right to disobey a plainly valid law? Can failing to register under the Selective Service Act or obstructing the shipment of munitions ever be socially or morally justified as a citizen's form of protest even though it is legally wrong? Can one distinguish between these cases and those of the sit-in demonstrators and others who engage in demonstrations for a just cause, knowing that they violate well-established laws, but uncertain whether those laws are constitutional? We sometimes have to leave the legal question to decision after the event, but surely the moral question must be faced in advance of action.

In answering the question we may put aside for the present the problems raised by men like Thoreau who reject society and go off by themselves into the wilderness eschewing demands upon other men which might yield a reciprocal social obligation. We are speaking now of those whose concern is to influence society through effective promotion of reform.

The examples of Socrates, Gandhi, and our more violent revolutionary forefathers are also distinguishable. Their challenge was to regimes which gave them neither the means of effectuating guarantees of liberty nor the political processes essential to effective self-government. Both the liberty and processes are available within our constitutional system. Were it not for the power of the Federal government to which he could turn for justice and equality within a framework of constitutionalism, the Negro might have offered a justification similar to Gandhi's, at least in the South where he was effectively disenfranchised and treated as an outcast.

For one who has personal liberty, the franchise, and freedom of political action, the question is altogether different. His civil disobedience may secure his goal or at least nudge society in that direction. If his goal is right and important, the accomplishment, taken by itself, may be significant, but surely a wise man would take a longer and broader view and ask the price to be paid for the possible accomplishment before striking the moral or social balance.

Let me pose the problem concretely as it arose not too long ago at a midwestern college. A paper company was planning to build a new mill in an Alabama community. The college was near one of its northern mills. The students who were interested in the civil rights movement, asked the company to promise not to build the southern mill unless the local officials in the Alabama community agreed to provide greater political and economic equality for Negroes. When the paper company refused, the students began picketing. The picketing soon turned into climbing all over the company's property, blocking entrances and exits, and otherwise physically disrupting its business by what was euphemistically called, I suppose, "nonviolent action." The company obtained a court injunction against the plainly unlawful trespasses. The students disobeyed the injunction and were cited for contempt. At that point the company gave in to the demands. The students' purpose had been deeply moral. They accomplished a thoroughly desirable objective, but I wonder whether that is the end of the question. Should we say that their conduct was morally justified because they followed the teachings of conscience, even though they flagrantly violated the law? Or should we say, on the other hand, that they were morally wrong because the impetus they gave to the cause of racial equality was not worth the cost in terms of the long-run damage they did to the rule of law?

Before you answer, consider whether you would say that the conduct of the students differed essentially from that of Governors Barnett and Wallace, when they disobeyed Federal court orders to admit Negroes to public schools. Could not the governors have as fairly argued that they were doing nothing more than exercising the right of protest through nonviolent, civil disobedience to what they regarded as the immoral fiat of nine justices seeking to impose their social views upon the country instead of following the established law of the constitution? To deny the bona fides of Governors Barnett and Wallace is only to evade the real question. Much as we may disagree, it is entirely possible for men to act as they did out of sincere moral conviction. There is no escape from weighing the costs as well as the justification for disobedience to the law.

One cost we pay for all civil disobedience is the heavy damage it does to the principle of government by consent of the governed — a principle which is the surest guaranty of individual liberty devised by man and also the source of the widest opportunities men have ever enjoyed to remake society without repeated violence in contests for physical or economic power. Repeated widespread disobedience to the law's commands therefore puts at hazard individual liberty, freedom of speech and association, and opportunities for peaceful change through a government responsive to the people.

Let me put the problem as I have felt its edge. From the standpoint of law the conduct of the students in the paper mill incident was just like that of the governors of Mississippi and Alabama in opposing school desegregation. Both, asserting a moral right of civil disobedience, defied judicial decrees. The moral standards of the governors, unlike those of the students, were wrong by any test, but, so far as I know, the governors honestly believed that they were right. Should they be condemned only because we differ from them on the morality of their objective? Who is to be the moral censor? And if each is to judge for himself, how can we avoid social chaos?

A related incident will further illustrate the point. About the same time that school desegregation came to a crisis in Alabama, the Supreme Court decided that to open the day in the public schools by reading from the Bible or saying a prayer violates the First and Fourteenth Amendments.[8] Governor Wallace announced that the teachers would continue to lead children in opening prayers and read from the Bible in the schools of Alabama. He challenged the Attorney General to enforce the Supreme Court's decision. Would you say that Governor Wallace and any schoolteachers in Alabama who persisted in the prayers and the Bible-reading were morally right? Assuming their sincerity in continuing with the prayers, theirs would have been nonviolent action to force a change in what they believed to be an immoral law. I doubt whether anyone will presume to say with certainty that the governor and the teachers who continued as a matter of conscience to lead the prayers and read the Bible could not sincerely believe in the morality of their objective. If they were sincere, their situation was no different from that of the students disobeying the injunction against trespassing at the paper mill. If they were morally right in continuing the prayers and Bible-reading despite the Supreme Court's decision, what should we say of those who might sit down in the school corridors or block the driveways to protest what they believed to be the great moral wrong of leading children to engage in religious exercises in

[8] Abington School District v. Schempp, 374 U.S. 203.

the public schools? Surely this group could be as conscientious as the first, and if the first had the moral right to defy the law, so did the second. I do not see how we can maintain schools — or ultimately how we can carry on an organized society — if everyone has a moral right to use civil disobedience to impose his will on the community without regard to the beliefs and rights of others, sanctioned by the law. Nor do I see how one can distinguish the disobedience of the constitutional command against establishment of religion from the disobedience of the command to give equal education to Negroes and whites in the public schools.

When Governor Wallace made his announcement that Alabama would disregard the Supreme Court's decisions in the school prayer and Bible-reading cases, the Attorney General called me in and asked what response he should make and whether I thought that he was required to send troops if necessary to enforce the Supreme Court's decision. I answered, "Of course not." Then he went on to say, "What should I do?" I could only murmur that the problem was a long way off, that there was no case actually involving Alabama, and that perhaps the question would never arise.

It was a lame answer but the incident illustrates better than any other in my experience the extent to which the rule of law depends upon voluntary compliance. Often there is no satisfactory answer to the question, how should the law be enforced. On some occasions there is no practical power, and on others no practical power we are willing to use, to enforce it. The former would have been true in 1952, when the Supreme Court invalidated President Truman's seizure of the steel mills, if the President had said, "I do not intend to comply with the Court's decision. I think that it is morally wrong." It would probably have been true in the summer of 1963 if the railroad workers had persisted by the thousands in going on strike, regardless of what statute Congress might enact or what decree a court might enter. The simple fact is that our constitutional system works and our society is free because officials, individuals, and the community realize that in the end the rule of law depends upon voluntary compliance. Such is the true meaning of government by consent of the governed. Voluntary compliance is essential to the rule of law.

I am not blind to the need for the coercive power of the State. The policeman's billy will be an indispensable part of every legal system until we reach the millennium. That swift enforcement can and must follow disobedience, even by a State against constitutional judgments, is evidenced by our early constitutional history as well as the more recent events in Mississippi and Alabama.[9] In cases affecting individuals, whether civil or criminal, the sheriff stands behind the court's decree. Nonetheless, even in the case of individuals, force can be invoked only in exceptional cases. It supports but cannot take the place of free assent, for in the final analysis force and the rule of law are antithetical. The core of the evil in true civil disobedience is that it weakens the bonds of law and compels the State to resort to power.

You may object that this is a lawyer's view and that if a law is truly unjust, there is no reason to preserve it. My answer is that we are concerned with the basic idea of law — with a force binding all men — and that you cannot pick and choose among good laws and bad laws according to each individual's conscience without destroying the whole concept of the rule of law. Nor do I attach value to the rule of law just because it is law. Law is a human instrument, constructed by men to meet men's needs; it must justify itself by what it does for men in meeting their needs, including their ethical judgments and moral aspirations. In this sense the rule

[9] Mississippi and Alabama were not the first to challenge the Supreme Court's constitutional adjudications. Pennsylvania in 1810, Virginia in 1816 and 1821, Kentucky in 1823, and Georgia in 1832 each breathed defiance but the challenge was met then as later by executive action.

of law—our constitutionalism—offers three ultimately moral justifications:

First, it secures for men the maximum of individual liberty, freedom of speech and association, religion and privacy, and equality before the law.

Second, it secures the greatest opportunities for peaceful change not only today but in the future.

Third, the ultimate commitment of those devoted to the rule of law is to the belief that the growth of each individual toward responsibility and the freedom to choose the best he can discern is a purpose which must never be made subservient to other objectives.

History reveals no substitute for the rule of law in fulfilling these purposes. Men can be lifted from savagery to a form of civilization solely through the pacification achieved by concentrating power in the hands of the State, but neither mere pacification nor the concentration of power will secure individual liberty and opportunities for each generation to remake society, if it can, without a violent revolution. To achieve these goals, even the power of the government must be restrained, and ways must be found by which men can live together not by power, be it physical, economic, or in some cases even political, but by what reason tells is just. To achieve both civility and freedom, with opportunities for change, there must be a substitute for power.

Our substitute is the rule of law. Our constitutionalism is founded upon seven or eight centuries of continuous concern for the institutions and aspirations — for the processes, standards, ideals, and sense of right and justice — that make for a free and civilized society organized with a minimum of force and a maximum of reason. Ours is a free society because the law binds all men equally, the governors as well as the governed, the judges as well as the litigants. Through the Bill of Rights, even the people, the ultimate rulers in a democracy, have voluntarily subjected themselves to the restraint of law, and they have created courts to help them observe the law's prohibitions.

It is the capacity to command free assent that makes law a substitute for power. The force of legitimacy — and conversely the habit of voluntary compliance — is the foundation of the law's civilizing and liberalizing influence. Indeed, I am prepared to insist that law in this sense is the very fabric of a free society. There is no alternative short of the millennium.

The damage may be great, as was threatened and partially done by the civil disobedience of Governors Barnett and Wallace, and as it would have been if President Truman had held the steel mills in defiance of the Supreme Court. It may be small, as when a student burns his draft card or disregards an injunction against physically obstructing the conduct of a lawful business. In either event, the damage is done, and the ultimate guaranty of freedom and peaceful change is just that much weaker.

When I speak of the rule of law, I mean not a static set of rules but a process. Law is a civilizing and liberating influence only so long as it arises out of the conditions of contemporary society and serves the current needs of men. The capacity for change and growth is as essential an element of the rule of law as reason and voluntary compliance. Indeed, voluntary compliance cannot be severed from the other side of the coin—to win consent of the governed the law must deserve acceptance. When the pace of social change or the growth of social conscience is revolutionary, so must be the changes in the law.

Social protest and even civil disobedience serve the law's need for growth. Ideally, reform would come according to reason and justice without self-help and disturbing, almost violent, forms of protest. Resort to such pressures is hardly consistent with the ideals of reason and civility. Those who use direct action eschew reason in favor of a form of force, whether it be economic power or simply the power to upset the community by interfering with its normal life. No little cause will justify their action. Still, candor compels one here again to acknowledge the gap between the ideal and the reality. Short of the millennium, sharp changes in the law depend partly upon the stimulus of protest.

History affords abundant examples. The extension of the rule of law to millions of workers in industrial establishments is one of the great creative accomplishments of law in the present century, but the stimulus came from strikes, boycotts, and picketing that, under the older precedents, were quite plainly illegal. Similarly, while we may take some measure of reassurance from the demonstrated capacity of our statutory, judge-made, and constitutional law to grow in response to demands for racial justice, that satisfaction must be tempered by the admission that for decades the law was blind to the wrongs and its eyes were opened only by picketing, boycotts, sit-ins, marches, and other demonstrations creating the specter of violence. The legality of the sit-ins and some of the marches was far from certain.

If what I have said thus far be true, even one with a conscience sensitive to the rule of law faces a dilemma. If he disobeys the existing rule established by statute or embodied in judicial decisions, he violates the precept of voluntary compliance, but if he obeys, he forgoes for himself and thereby deprives all of us of the chance that the law will change, and that, under the impact of his action, it will be decided that what he did was actually legal, despite the contrary precedents, either because it did not violate the relevant statutes or rules of decision or else because it involved the exercise of a constitutional right.

Under such circumstances one can hardly lump together all conduct potentially involving civil disobedience and then brand it, in terms of conscience, as altogether right or altogether wrong. On the contrary, one can say with considerable assurance that the test is not always whether the action taken is consistent with the rights of others under existing rules and finds sanction in existing precedents. Surely there is a difference between (1) those who resort to self-help and other nonviolent action in disobedience to civil authority conscientiously believing that what they are doing involves the exercise of a legal right as the courts will declare it and (2) those who violate a plainly valid law knowing that their conduct is illegal.

The first group would seem to do no moral wrong merely because their conduct turns out to be illegal. The law, as made by judges, grows and changes in response to what is done by those strong enough to assert new rights in the face of existing precedents. A good example is the march from Selma to Montgomery. The march went on for five days, necessitated closing half an important highway, caused innumerable traffic jams, cost $500,000 in pay for the National Guardsmen, and, but for the show of military force, would have precipitated serious violence and disorder. Conventional views of the First Amendment based upon prior decisions would have permitted the authorities to prohibit so massive a demonstration in order to serve the interests of the community in law enforcement, traffic control, the avoidance of tensions, and ordered liberty. Under the pressure of events Judge Frank Johnson laid down the novel but sound principle that "[the] extent of the right to assemble, demonstrate and march peaceably along the highways and streets in an orderly manner should be commensurate with the enormity of the wrongs that are being protested and petitioned against."[10] Judge Johnson found the wrongs to be "enormous," and the extent of the right to demonstrate was determined accordingly.

The civil disobedience of the sit-in demonstrators also belongs in this category, although perhaps their action was illegal. Judged by then existing law, they

[10] Williams v. Wallace, 240 F. Supp. 100, 106.

were trespassing against the settled rights of the operators of restaurants and lunch counters, and their constitutional challenge went far beyond the precedents. Their grievance, however, was greater than any other in the community, reason and civility had yielded no response, and their legal argument that the Fourteenth Amendment gave them a direct constitutional right to equal service at restaurants and lunch counters was not without an honest and substantial hope of success.[11] The legality of their conduct has never been finally adjudicated, but I would not question its morality on the ground that it might have turned out to be illegal. Of course, to have continued the same course of conduct once the point was adjudicated would present an entirely different situation.

What I have said does not imply that disobedience of the commands of local authorities is always morally justified provided it may be found to involve the exercise of a constitutional right. Happily, the law is providing an increasing number of methods for obtaining an advance judicial determination of constitutional questions affecting First Amendment freedoms.[12] Society would disintegrate if demonstrations and direct action widely replaced reason and

[11] The argument is best stated in the concurring opinion of Justice Douglas in Lombard v. Louisiana, 373 U.S. 267, 274, and of Justice Goldberg in Bell v. Maryland, 378 U.S. 226, 286.

[12] E.g., Dombrowski v. Pfister, 380 U.S. 479.

civility as methods of resolving questions of public policy. Repeated resort to such tactics is also likely to lessen their usefulness when truly needed. Nevertheless, when the cause is just, when there is urgency, and when other channels are closed, we should defend the social and moral right to disobey a law that one sincerely believes will be held unconstitutional, even though he turns out to be wrong. Whatever harm is done to the principle of consent is balanced by the need to conform the law to the demands of conscience.

When we come to the second group, those who are disregarding a plainly valid law—a law plainly valid because its meaning and constitutionality could not honestly be doubted or because the courts have already entered a judgment declaring the actor's duty—then the situation seems quite different. The best examples are those of Governors Barnett and Wallace, the students climbing on the paper mill, and other such forms of obstruction of the daily business of society as sitting down in public offices and refusal to pay taxes or, for political reasons, to register for the draft. In such cases three observations seem pertinent.

First, this method of protest can rarely be justified by the Socratic or Ghandian defense of disobedience to laws which in conscience should not be obeyed because they are unjust. There is nothing unjust about a law that requires tourists to keep moving on a visit to the White House or forbids students from disrupting the work in a Selective Service office or in the Department of Justice; nor is there anything unjust about laws that prohibit people from lying on the runways in airports to make it impossible for planes to land or take off or blocking streets or interfering with the free movement of trains. Compliance with such laws requires one neither to do nor submit to an injustice.

Second, in such cases and in a number of others, there is a lack of any real relationship between the act of protest and what is being protested against. In the Freedom Rides and the sit-in demonstrations, the demonstrators were seeking equality of treatment directly instead of by lawsuit. This kind of relationship does not exist in the case of the tactics I have just mentioned or in such instances as the refusal to pay taxes because of some remote connection between the taxes paid and the nature of some government expenditure.

Third, even when there is a close relationship, if the illegality is plain—if no careful lawyer could conscientiously tell a client that the direct action might be found legal—then the teaching of conscience as well as of law would ordinarily seem to call for compliance until change is achieved by constitutional process. Here representative government affords the opportunity to secure redress of grievances, and the constitution secures enormously wide opportunities to speak, publicize, persuade, and demonstrate without undermining the force of law.

Possibly there are a few rare occasions on which the goal would be so important and so plainly right as to outweigh the price which a challenge to the rule of law exacts from the community. I know of none today. The argument is probably strongest where one refuses to do what he believes is a direct moral wrong to others. In all other cases, it would seem to me that the man who is willing to damage the processes of constitutionalism, which guarantee liberty and the chance of repeated change without force, in order to impose his views upon society, must be either peculiarly self-confident or extremely shortsighted.

Even then the wrong is not the challenge to existing society. Past generations have made a mess of things, ours no less than our fathers'. The hope of mankind is always that a new generation may begin to make the world over quickly. The wrong, in the simplest terms, is the damage to the foundation upon which rests the best, if not the only real, opportunity for the making-over.

Federalism and Civil Rights

MARK DeWOLFE HOWE

NINETY-FOUR YEARS AGO the junior Senator from Indiana addressed the conscience of the Nation when he discussed the course which untamed violence had recently taken in the South: "It is a reproach to the Republic and a confession of its failure as a Government, that such things may occur, not once or occasionally, as might happen under the best Government, but habitually and for months in succession. . . . Where, today, in any government laying claim to be a civilized one, are such outrages enacted with impunity as are borne to us on every breeze which comes from the South?"[1] The southerlies are still blowing. They have told us of the killing of Medgar Evers, William Moore, James Reeb, Andrew Goodman, James Chaney, Michael Schwerner, Lemuel Penn, Viola Liuzzo, and Jonathan Daniels. They brought us the names of others, but those others we have forgotten because they were merely four little children at church in Birmingham. The breezes from the South have told us these ugly tales, but they have not spoken of convictions of the guilty. They tell us, instead, of murders, acquittals, mistrials, and local pride.

My purpose here is not to arouse your indignation. The task which I have set myself is that of identify-

---

[1] Remarks of Senator Pratt, April 6, 1871, *Congressional Globe*, 42nd Cong., 1st Sess., p. 504.

ing and comprehending the concept which, above all others, has served to incapacitate the Nation's conscience. I mean, in other words, to look rather closely at certain aspects of American federalism — at elements in constitutional history that seem to me to have been overlooked. The inquiry, I fear, will lead me into that forest which frightens and repels so many Americans — even American historians — the dark woodlands of American legal history. I cannot, however, conceal my conviction that the shape of our moral expectations, like the structure of our political capacities, has been much affected by the legal setting in which the expectations were born and bred.

The story that concerns me begins with the familiar pronouncement of Lord Mansfield, uttered on the King's Bench in 1772: "The state of slavery . . . is so odious, that nothing can be suffered to support it, but positive law."[2] This emancipating dictum was, of course, woven into a confused pattern of contradictory traditions and practices. One tradition (or was it merely a slogan?) asserted that "England was too pure an air for slaves to breath in."[3] Yet imperial Britain was quite willing to encourage the slave trade between Africa and her American plantations,

[2]The Case of James Sommersett, 20 How State Trials 2, 82 (1772).
[3] Quoted in Catterall, *Judicial Cases concerning American Slavery and the Negro* (Washington, 1926), I, 1.

and English courts of common law were quite ready to respect the positive law of any colony that chose to establish or to uphold slavery. Surely it is not surprising that the American heirs of such a confused tradition could in southern plantations maintain, and in northern colonies disclaim, the institutions of slavery. In these matters, as in many other aspects of our social order, it is important to remember that in the house of Anglo-American law there have been many mansions. At the close of the eighteenth century, English and American lawyers found nothing strange in a pronouncement that while the common law of England and the law of nature condemn slavery, positive law and the law of nations sustain it.

This pluralistic character of the laws of England was not unimportant to the Justices of the Supreme Judicial Court of Massachusetts when they came in 1783 to consider the status of slavery in the Commonwealth. Much has been written on the Quock Walker case, and of the charge delivered to the jury by Chief Justice Cushing.[4] Acknowledging that slavery had been countenanced by provincial statute, Cushing emphasized that it had never been ex-

[4] See, e.g., John D. Cushing, "The Cushing Court and the Abolition of Slavery in Massachusetts," *American Journal of Legal History*, 5 (1961), 118.

pressly brought into being by legislative action and that it had no firmer sanction than that of usage. Whether or not the Chief Justice thought that custom and usage constituted "positive law" within the meaning of that phrase as Lord Mansfield had used it, we do not know. In any case, the Chief Justice was unwilling to let the institution survive under a Constitution that proclaimed equality and promised liberty. I might add that Wendell Phillips and Lemuel Shaw seem to me to have spoken quite accurately when they asserted that Lord Mansfield's dictum with respect to the dependency of slavery upon positive law made usage and custom no less effective instruments for sustaining the infamous institution than did statutes.[5]

This pluralistic inheritance has, I believe, a greater significance in American constitutional history than has commonly been recognized. Statesmen and scholars have often called our attention to the awkward and embarrassed circumlocutions by which the framers of the Federal Constitution made reference to the ugly fact of slavery. An anonymous pamphleteer in 1819 wrote of "that policy of virtuous shame which sought to shadow our internal condi-

[5] Phillips, *Review of Lysander Spooner's Essay on the Unconstitutionality of Slavery* (Boston, 1847), pp. 84-85; Shaw, C. J., in Commonwealth v. Aves, 18 Pick. 193, 212 (1836).

tion in a constitution destined for the study and admiration of the world."[6] What the commentator had in mind, of course, were those coward's clauses that dared not speak of slaves but spoke instead of persons "held to service or labor" and, with something less than candor, contrasted "free persons," not with Negro slaves, but with "all other persons."[7] I have no doubt that the desire to shadow our shame from European inspection played some part in these evasions. I think that it is clear, however, that they were also designed by the lawyers to fit the law of the Constitution to the law that Lord Mansfield had so recently proclaimed. If slavery gets its life from positive law—from constitution, statute, custom, or usage—it was important to those who longed for the institution's early end that the Constitution should say nothing that would give it "positive" endorsement. It was no less unlikely that the foes of slavery would accept a document that provided explicit sanctions for safeguarding and preserving the institution than that South Carolina and Georgia would ratify a Constitution that contemplated its outlawry by national authority. What the Nation needed, accord-

---

[6] *Free Remarks on the Spirit of the Federal Constitution, the Practice of the Federal Government, and the Obligations of the Union Respecting the Exclusion of Slavery from the Territories and New States by a Philadelphian* (Philadelphia, 1819), p. 20.

[7] Art. IV, Sec. 2, paragraph 3; Art. I, Sec. 2, paragraph 3.

ingly, was what the Nation had inherited — a British pluralism in law if not in morals — a tolerance sufficiently generous to allow slavery in the South and permit abolition in the North.

One word more is needed, I fear, if I am to set the scene for the later events of our constitutional history. You will remember that English aphorisms with respect to freedom have, in one form or another, reiterated the principle that the common law of England is so permeated by the spirit of liberty as to make slavery intolerable. If that common law is our inheritance, as the founding patriots constantly asserted it to be, how can the Nation's government at once preserve the inheritance and the slavery? The classic answer, being technical, is not wholly satisfying, but it must, I fear, be accepted. It consists in the reminder that there is no common law of the United States. The law of the Nation contains no other elements than those provided by the Constitution and by the statutes enacted by the Congress. This classic principle is important for my present purpose, because it underlines the fact that if the Constitution and statutes of the Nation before the Civil War preserved a deep and silent neutrality with respect to slavery, there was no other law of the Nation that could speak to the issue that divided the minds and the hearts of the American people.

This analysis suggests that the shame that shadowed our condition was the by-product of British pluralism—the consequence of a system of law ingeniously designed to allow the survival of an institution that the King's justices in some circumstances sustained, but in all circumstances branded a violation of the law of nature and intolerable by the standards of the common law. While our federalism embraced enough of this disorder in principle to permit South Carolina to have her slavery and Massachusetts her freedom, our Federal judges were denied the consoling jurisdiction of the common law—the capacity occasionally to circumvent a positive law of servitude by enforcing a common law of freedom. This Nation's commitment to silence on the largest issue that confronted the American people was at once a distinctive and a startling contribution to the art of government. Though war, constitutional amendments, and economic revolution have vastly altered the structure and the content of American law, the old commitment to national silence and national disability still serves to make American federalism a significant impediment to the fulfillment of civil rights.

In what I have said of the constitutional commitment to incapacity I am afraid that I have given too much attention to the role of judges. The decision of the framers of the Constitution that the domestic destiny of slavery was to be in the hands of the States and not in those of the Nation meant, of course, that the Congress should not by positive law sustain slavery, or by negative law end it. I have sometimes wondered whether the framers might not most accurately have expressed their determination to keep the congressional hands off all problems of slavery by adopting a provision modeled upon the neutralities of the First Amendment—a provision stating, in effect, that "Congress shall make no law establishing slavery or prohibiting the enslavement of Negroes." Some such prohibition as that would, I believe, have made explicit the tacit negations of the Constitution. It would have served to accentuate the conviction of the framers that if the Nation should seek to deal either sympathetically or antagonistically with the institution of slavery the frail bonds of union would burst apart.

May I pause in my hurried passage through time to call your attention to the peculiar brand of federalism which these silences and disabilities brought into being? We generally suppose that the central problems of federalism concern the relationships that prevail between the Nation and the States— that the crucial issues in making the constitution of a Federal society effective relate to defining the scope of national and State power. Classic examples of such issues I should take to be the determination of the range and significance of congressional power to regulate commerce among the several States, and the definition of the limits of the States to tax instrumentalities of the Federal government. To cite those examples is to dramatize the very different character of the issue of federalism as it related to the institution of slavery. Starting with the dominant presupposition that the Nation had no power of any sort to touch the institution of domestic slavery, the American courts soon discovered that problems of federalism as they bore on slavery did not concern the relationships of States to Nation but the relationships of States to one another. Could South Carolina imprison free Negroes serving as seamen on Massachusetts vessels in Charleston?[8] Could Massachusetts give freedom to slaves who were brought by their masters from Louisiana to enjoy a cool summer in the Bay Commonwealth?[9] There being no Federal common law of freedom and no congressional positivism establishing slavery, there was simply a conflict of laws to be resolved in

[8] See Elkison v. Deliesseline, 1 Brunner 431; Fed. Cas. No. 4366 (1823).
[9] Commonwealth v. Aves, 18 Pick. 193 (1836).

the courts of the several States, and a conflict of principles to be resolved by the churches throughout the land. The Nation's judges, the Nation's legislators were powerless to resolve either of those conflicts.

Doubtless the learned minds of some of my readers are troubled by my failure, so far, to say anything of the implications in those evasive phrases in Article Four that dealt with fugitive slaves. This ingenious circumlocution of the framers deserves quotation: "No person held to service or labor in one State, under the laws thereof, escaping into another, shall, in consequence of any law or regulation therein, be discharged from such service or labor, but shall be delivered up on claim of the party to whom such service or labor may be due." If you look behind the shadows cast by those shamefaced words you will see the commitment that came to outrage the abolitionists — the assurance that the United States Constitution saw masters of men as owners of property. If we ask ourselves whether the constitutional assurance with respect to fugitive slaves provided that sort of recognition of slavery by positive law which Mansfield said sufficed to sustain it, our answer, I fear, will depend upon our moral presuppositions. On its face the provision seems to reflect one supposition — the assumption that issues with respect to the rendition of fugitive slaves must be resolved by interstate arrangements. Nothing in the language of the provision quoted from Article Four suggests that the Congress was empowered to impose duties upon the custodian of the fugitive to restore him to his master. Every settled principle of interpretation supports the thesis of Charles Sumner and Chancellor Walworth that the fugitive-slave clause of the Constitution, in the eyes of the framers, was to find its enforcement in the good faith of the States and not in the strong arm of the Nation.[10] The provision, in other words, reflected the basic constitutional assumption that I have emphasized—the supposition that the destiny of slavery within and between the States was to be determined by their law and not by the laws of the United States.

The Congress in 1793 and the Supreme Court in 1842 rejected the constitutional thesis that Sumner urged in his day and that I once more support as well-grounded. The Second Congress in February, 1793, adopted An Act Respecting Fugitives from Justice and [Respecting] Persons Escaping from the Service of Their Masters[11]—a statute which had a

[10] Charles Sumner, "Freedom National; Slavery Sectional," *Works of Sumner* (Boston, 1871), III, 95, 147 *et seq.;* Walworth, C., in Jack v. Martin, 14 Wendell 507, 524, 525-528 (1835).

[11] 1 Stat. 302.

somewhat surprising and tragic career when it came into the hands of the judges. The statute's first sections—whose which dealt with fugitives from justice—were held by Chief Justice Taney to subject the officials in the state of refuge to no other than moral obligations to surrender the fugitive.[12] Yet a majority of the Court, with Taney concurring, held in *Prigg* v. *Pennsylvania* that the sections of the statute that dealt with fugitive slaves not only were constitutional but subjected those persons who sheltered fugitive slaves to a legal obligation to restore them to their owners.[13]

I will not put your patience to the strain of following the details of an argument that seems to me to sustain Sumner's thesis that the congressional effort to require the rendition of fugitive slaves was unconstitutional. Lawful or unlawful, the power was exercised and it was sustained. In that exercise of power the Congress broke the silence which the framers had endeavored to guarantee. A positive law sustaining one aspect of slavery had been enacted by the Congress and had been so interpreted by the Court as to involve the planting of the seeds of a new nationalism. From that first and almost casual endorsement of slavery there grew, of course,

[12] Kentucky v. Dennison, 24 How. 66 (1861).
[13] Prigg v. Pennsylvania, 16 Peters 539 (1842).

the searing controversies of the 1840's and '50's with respect to the rendition of Anthony Burns, Thomas Sims, and all the other refugees from slavery. One element in this chapter from the history of the relationships between federalism and civil rights deserves special emphasis. I have suggested that the constitutional offense which the Congress committed in 1793 — and which the Court endorsed in 1842 — was its creation of a Federal obligation to fulfill a responsibility which the Constitution had left in the exclusive jurisdiction of the States. Let me remind you once more of certain language in the section of Article Four that deals with fugitive slaves. "No person held to service ... in one State, ... escaping into another, shall, *in consequence of any law or regulation therein,* be discharged from such service." No one who is willing to accept the supremacy of the Federal Constitution over State law could, I take it, seriously question the unconstitutionality under this provision of any State statute that purported to emancipate fugitive slaves. Using the language of today's constitutional law one can accurately assert that the provision in Article Four that I have quoted deals with and prohibits State action. Despite that fact, when the Second Congress in 1793 adopted its statute on fugitive slaves, it showed no hesitation to impose criminal liability upon private persons who hindered the rendition of fugitives. In *Prigg* v. *Pennslyvania* the Supreme Court found no great difficulty in legitimating the congressional control of private action that served to frustrate claims of slaveholders and prevent the State of refuge from fulfilling its constitutional responsibilities.[14]

The Court's determination in the Prigg case that nothing in the Federal structure of our government precludes the Congress from fully safeguarding private rights derived from the Constitution seems to me wholly unexceptionable. To say that, however, is not to endorse the Court's accompanying decision that the Congress was empowered to enact positive law in support of slavery. The recognition of that power constituted, in my judgment, the repudiation of a studied and elaborate effort of the framers to produce a national authority that on one matter should be voiceless. Perhaps Justice Story and his associates had come to believe that the effort of the framers had been born in innocence and had been nurtured in false hope and, therefore, could no

---

[14] Daniel Webster, in 1850, expressed doubts concerning the Court's willingness to find constitutional justification for congressional control of private action in a prohibition of State action. See *Works of Daniel Webster* (Boston, 1856), V, 354.

longer be permitted to govern the Nation's destiny. The decision, however, that slavery henceforth would be sustained not merely by interstate comity but by national authority brought an end to the old federalism – the close of the era of silence and disability.

If constitutional law had terminated with *Prigg* v. *Pennsylvania*, scholars and lawyers could confidently assert that there is nothing in the nature of American federalism that disables the Congress from controlling private conduct affecting the civil rights of others. Yet after a Civil War that preserved the Union, after constitutional amendments that abolished slavery, promised equal protection of the laws to Negroes and specifically empowered Congress to make the assurances of the amendments effective, we find ourselves somehow committed to the doctrine that American federalism outlaws congressional legislation directed against private acts of violence that are designed, through terror, to frustrate the fulfillment of the Nation's promise. Let me now try to trace a few neglected strands in the unhappy progression from pre-War power to post-War impotence.

When the Congress proposed and the States ratified the Thirteenth Amendment, the people announced their decision that slavery should no longer exist in the United States.[15] Experience had taught us that a nation cannot avoid the responsibility of decision—that the dream of the framers that somehow the United States need make no commitment for or against slavery was shattered. It seemed wise, therefore, not only that there should be a constitutional outlawry of slavery, but that Congress should be explicitly empowered to make the outlawry totally effective. The second section of the Thirteenth Amendment provided, accordingly, that the Congress should have power to enforce the constitutional prohibition.

Within a few months after the amendment became effective, the Congress, exercising the powers thus newly conferred upon it, adopted the Civil Rights Act of 1866.[16] The statute, passed over the veto of Andrew Johnson, was written by men who were thoroughly familiar with the old problems of law to which I have directed your attention—the problems, that is, that Lord Mansfield had endeavored to resolve in 1772 and that American judges

[15]"Section 1. Neither slavery nor involuntary servitude, except as a punishment for crime whereof the party shall have been duly convicted, shall exist within the United States, or any place subject to their jurisdiction." "Section 2. Congress shall have power to enforce this article by appropriate legislation."
[16]14 Stat. 27.

had wrestled with for nearly a century. Had the slavery that was now being overthrown been born of common law, of international law, of custom, or of usage? Whatever its sources might have been the Congress wanted to make sure that the institution and the badges of inferiority with which it had degraded the Negro should be wholly eradicated. Accordingly the equality act of 1866 in its first section decreed that Negro citizens of the United States should henceforth be entitled to the same rights with respect to property, contracts, and inheritance that were enjoyed by white citizens. This assurance was explicitly to be made effective notwithstanding "any law, statute, ordinance, regulation, or custom to the contrary." The second section of the statute went on to make it a criminal offense for any person "under color of any law, statute, regulation, or custom" to deprive anyone of the rights of equality guaranteed by the first section.

Read in the context of the pluralism that I have described, the meaning of these statutory prohibitions takes on, I believe, a very different significance from that which they have generally been given. The Congress was not, I suggest, seeking to make it a Federal offense for State officials to deny equality of rights to Negro citizens. Instead, it was seeking to make it a crime for private persons, acting under the aura of a system outlawed by the Thirteenth Amendment, to persist in their discriminatory ways. Before emancipation no one who held Negroes in slavery had been able, with confidence, to say whether or not the holding was by virtue of law or by virtue of custom. A Congress that was anxious to prohibit the anticipated effort of white Southerners to keep alive their old advantages quite naturally supposed that it could undercut that effort by saying that those who denied equality under color of local laws or local customs that the Nation had now, in its new positivism, repudiated would be guilty of crime.

Many of you will remember that Andrew Johnson's unsuccessful veto of the equality act of 1866 stimulated some persons in the Congress to make their own confidence in its constitutionality doubly sure by proposing an additional amendment to the Constitution—that which became the Fourteenth. That amendment, you will recall, prohibited the States from impairing the privilege of citizenship, from depriving persons of life, liberty, or property without due process of law, and from denying persons the equal protection of the laws.

I have sometimes played with the paradoxical thought that this effort to assure Negro citizens that what they had been promised by the Thirteenth Amendment and the act of 1866 would really and truly be theirs was ultimately the source of their undoing. The paradox has this much truth. When the bits and pieces that constituted the Fourteenth Amendment were put together it included a prohibition of State denials of equal protection of the laws. The provision seems, on its face, to legitimate the equality act of 1866. What no one seems to have contemplated, however, at the time of reinforcement, was that the meaning of the statute might acquire a very different shading from the sweeping prohibitions of the Fourteenth Amendment than from the more specific interdictions of the Thirteenth. Remember that whereas the latter secures a few rights against the whole world, the Fourteenth Amendment safeguards an almost unlimited number of rights primarily against a very few persons — those who represent the State. The statutory condemnation of discriminations under color of law or usage, read in the context of the Thirteenth Amendment, seems to outlaw all conduct, public and private, designed to keep alive the degradations that were rooted in the laws and customs of slavery. The same condemnation, read in the context of the Fourteenth Amendment, may seem to reach no other discriminations than those enforced by officials exercising the State's powers. In 1870 the Congress transposed the equality act of 1866 into the center of a new Civil Rights Act that afforded protection for rights conferred by the Fourteenth and Fifteenth Amendments.[17] That transfer, not surprisingly, led courts and lawyers to forget the statute's Thirteenth Amendment paternity and to see it as the fruit of the powers conferred on Congress by the Fourteenth Amendement. Thus there came into being the assumption that the presuppositions of the Fourteenth Amendment confined the reach of the equality act to official denials of equality.

Where has this search for meaning taken me? What the story suggests is that the framers of the Thirteenth Amendment and the draftsmen of the act of 1866 were willing to have the Congress outlaw any private discriminations against Negroes that were traceable to the institutions of slavery. It does not seem to me surprising that a generation which recalled the frustrations of a federalism that had endeavored to sanctify national disability should consider it time for a national government to be established. I have not seen any evidence that when the Fourteenth Amendment was adopted its framers intended to take back any of the congressional authority which the Thirteenth Amendment had created — the authority, that is, to deal with private

[17] Sections 16 and 17 of the Civil Rights Act of May 31, 1870, 16 Stat. 140, 144.

efforts to perpetuate the inequalities born of slavery. Nor is there, in my judgment, persuasive evidence to suggest that the congressional power specifically granted in the Fourteenth Amendment to enforce its prohibitions of State action was intended merely to authorize legislative condemnations of practices that the amendment's own prohibitions outlawed. I see very little reason, in other words, to believe that the Fourteenth Amendment denied Congress the power to condemn private action designed either to impair the privileges of the colored citizens of the United States or to prevent the States from safeguarding the liberty and equality of Negroes.

Before I briefly consider the paradoxical fallout from the liberating promises of the Fourteenth Amendment, I must pause to ask what contribution the Civil War amendments made to the progress of American federalism. If I am right in my suggestion that the Nation's pre-War constitutional commitment to silence and disability was not the reflection of a general philosophy with respect to federalism but the consequence of our pluralistic inheritance with respect to slavery, then it would seem that the Thirteenth Amendment's breaking of silence—its resounding renunciation of the old neutrality— should have served to release the Nation's powers so that they might be applied to outlaw the indecencies of racial discrimination. Of course the general principles of federalism would still operate to make inadvisable—perhaps even unconstitutional—the needless or abusive exercise of national power over matters of primarily local concern. But the restraints derived from such general principles as those are surely less disabling than those that had been born of the old specific commitment to incapacity with respect to slavery. In 1866 any prophet other than a visionary cynic would have assumed that if, in the old period of promised silence and neutrality, the Federal government could effectuate the rendition of fugitive slaves, in the new period of affirmation and commitment, it could take charge of their emancipation. Yet within twenty years after the War it became clear that the post-War Congress could do less to assure freedom than the pre-War Congress had done to safeguard slavery.

To uncover the forces that encouraged the revival of national disability would require an analysis of logic, law, and politics beyond my competence hastily to develop. I shall not, accordingly, seek to perform that task here. All that I can do is suggest that a crucial element in the resurrection of the old federalism was the almost unlimited sweep of the language of the Fourteenth Amendment. We know that its draftsmen were predominantly, if not wholly, concerned with assuring the total fulfillment of the promises of the Thirteenth Amendment and of the equality act of 1866. Yet the words that they selected to embrace this assurance made so many promises to so many persons that a cautious judiciary was not entirely wrongheaded, when the time for interpretation came, in seeking restrictive elements in the American tradition which could be used to confine the reach of national power.[18] If the Court had read the Fourteenth Amendment to authorize congressional protection of the lives, liberties, properties, and equalities of all persons against private injury, it would have given its blessing to a revolution much more radical than even abolitionists had demanded.

Had the Fourteenth Amendment specifically confined its prohibitions to racial discriminations, the Court might have been more tolerant of congressional control of private action. It might, accordingly, have acknowledged that Congress could make social discriminations in places of public accommodation unlawful in any State that did not fulfill its constitutional duty to outlaw them. The fear that

[18] Probably the cases that did most to discover restrictive traditions were the Slaughterhouse Cases, 16 Wall. 36 (1873) and The Civil Rights Cases, 109 U.S. 3 (1883).

under the Fourteenth Amendment, as it was in fact adopted, the Congress might not only seek to enact such legitimate laws as that but might endeavor to assure all persons security of person and property was not entirely unreasonable. In any case the fear contributed to the Court's determination that the reach of the amendment should be confined to those injuries that were done under the authority, real or apparent, of the State. From that determination derives today's uncertainty whether the Nation has power to punish those persons who killed our neighbors to prevent them from being our equals.

Does this return to my starting place bring me back with nothing more useful than indignation? I hope not. It seems to me that if the suggestions that I have offered have merit, they indicate that with a somewhat fuller consideration of the roots of our asserted disability its extent diminishes. It would indicate, in the first place, that the Congress is still vested with the power conferred upon it by the Thirteenth Amendment — the power, that is, to extirpate the vestiges of slavery. It indicates, furthermore, that the Congress should be permitted to seek the fulfillment of the predominant promise of the three Civil War amendments. That promise was that henceforth the Nation's authority would so be exercised as to subdue law's inhumanity to man. From the lesson of our first era of national disability we learned that a neutral government is a participant in the inhumanities of its citizens. Surely today it takes no stretch of constitutional power to exercise the Nation's authority over acts of racial terror and violence in communities that have rejected the supreme law of the land and encouraged hatred to go at large.

The Press and
the Courts

J. R. WIGGINS

Even as I am grateful for an opportunity to take a close and critical look at the coverage which the press gives to the courts, so I am sensible of the fact that this re-examination has driven me to conclusions that some will deplore. Certainly what I now have to say will be regarded by many as excessively critical of my own profession, my own colleagues, and even my own newspaper—for I have been led straight to the opinion that the press deserves a great deal of criticism for the way that it habitually covers the courts, particularly the lower courts. And its record is not good in relation to its coverage of any part of the governmental apparatus devoted to the detection of crime, the arrest of suspected persons, the indictment of accused persons, their trial, their acquittal or conviction, or their punishment or probation.

The plain truth of the matter is that the newspapers do not print enough crime news; they do not follow closely enough the conduct of the police, the operation of the courts, the administration of penal institutions, the functioning of the probation system—or any other aspects of society's handling of the whole enormous problem of crime.

Now if this indictment is valid, this is a very grave defect in the press, because the administration of justice in the United States greatly depends upon the continuous and close scrutiny by the press of the courts and the whole law enforcement system.

James Bryce in his great book *The American Commonwealth,* published in 1893, found that the courts in the United States were afflicted by grave weaknesses which much disturbed him. But he thought these weaknesses in part redeemed by the influence upon the courts of public opinion and the full reporting of judicial proceedings. After discussing the defects in our courts he asked why these structural faults had not produced correspondingly grave results. And he found three reasons for it. One was the coexistence of State and Federal courts. Another was the influence of the bar. And he said:

"Another is the influence of a public opinion which not only recognizes the interest the community has in an honest administration of the law, but recoils from turpitude in a highly placed official. The people act as a check upon the party conventions that choose candidates, by making them feel that they damage themselves and their cause if they run a man of doubtful character, and the judge himself is made to dread public opinion in the criticisms of a very reticent press. Democratic theory, which has done a mischief in introducing the elective system, partly cures it by subjecting the bench to the light of publicity which makes honesty the safest policy.

J. R. WIGGINS

Whatever passes in court is, or may be reported. The judge must give his reasons for every judgment he delivers."[1]

A long tradition, of course, lies behind the firm belief in this country that the courts must be openly conducted. There is wide acceptance of the theory enunciated by the Lord Chief Justice of England: "...justice must not only be done but most manifestly be seen to be done."[2] In the words of Lord Acton: "Everything secret degenerates, even the administration of justice; nothing is safe that does not show it can bear discussion and publicity."[3]

The impact of the open courtroom upon judicial proceedings has been attested by most of the great law writers. Its greatest import, of course, is on the quality of testimony. Professor John Henry Wigmore said it had the effect of "producing in the witnesses' mind a disinclination to falsity" in the presence of spectators who might be ready to "scorn a demonstrated liar."[4] Blackstone emphasized that a

[1] James Bryce, *The American Commonwealth*, (New York: The Macmillan Co., 1893), p. 508.
[2] Rex v. Justices of Bodmin, (1947) 1 K.B. 321, 325.
[3] Abbot Gasquet Oed, *Lord Acton and His Circle* (London: Burns and Oates, 1906), p. 166.
[4] John Henry Wigmore, *Treatise on the Anglo-American System of Evidence in Trials at Common Law* (Boston: Little, Brown and Co., 1940), VI, 1835.

"witness may frequently depose that, in private, which he will be ashamed to testify in a public and solemn tribunal."[5] As Bentham put it: "Environed as he sees himself, by a thousand eyes, contradiction, should he hazard a false tale, will seem ready to rise up in opposition from a thousand mouths."[6]

It is well known that the open court, besides improving the quality of testimony by known witnesses, may bring forth other witnesses. And public proceedings, as Bentham and Wigmore have most emphatically pointed out, keep the judge, while trying, under trial. Benthan thought that "without publicity, all other checks are insufficient; in comparison with publicity, all other checks are of small account."

Bentham also thought that open trials educated citizens as to their rights under the law. "By publicity," he said, "the temple of justice adds to its other functions that of a school, . . . a school of the highest order, where the most important branches of morality are enforced by the most impressive means, . . . a theatre in which the sports of the imagi-

[5] Sir William Blackstone, *Commentaries on the Laws of England* (London: W. Strahan, T. Cadell and D. Prince, 1783), p. 373.

[6] Jeremy Bentham, *Rationale of Judicial Evidence* (London: Hunt and Clark, 1827), IV, 317.

nation give place to the more interesting exhibitions of real life."[7]

Now, of course, in large part, these benefits of the open court theoretically are generally available in this country. Notwithstanding some State court opinions that an open trial is a right of the accused only, preponderant belief is that the open trial in addition serves other purposes of the sort dwelt upon by Blackstone, Bentham, Acton, Wigmore, and Cooley. But if these benefits are theoretically available, they are no longer, in any practical sense, as readily available as once they were. In the essentially rural society in which our system originated, the proceedings of the courts were watched very attentively indeed. Citizens flocked to the county seat during court sessions and by their very presence provided a scrutiny of the whole process. But urbanization has removed the courts far from the citizenry. The courtrooms today, in large urban centers, are not crowded with the generality of the citizenry. And if the citizens as a whole are to have any knowledge at all of what is going on in their lower courts, they are going to have to acquire it through the press.

But in our large urban centers, the sheer volume of business proceedings through the criminal courts

[7] *Rational of Judicial Evidence* (Bowing's Edition, 1843), Vol. II.

is so great that the overwhelming majority of these cases proceed through the courts with only the most casual attention by the press—and by the public. The press of this volume in Washington, I think, is quite typical of that in other cities. The size of the court establishment in our large cities almost defies the scrutiny of the public or the press. In the District of Columbia, this establishment, below the United States Supreme Court, includes the U. S. Court of Appeals, with nine judges; the U. S. District Court, with fifteen judges; the D. C. Court of Appeals, with three judges; the Court of General Sessions, with fifteen judges; and the Juvenile Court, with three judges. In addition, there are the Court of Military Appeals, the Court of Customs and Patent Appeals, the Tax Court, and the Court of Claims.

If The Washington *Post* were to cover all these courts with the purpose of telling its readers as much about their proceedings as they could find out for themselves as court spectators, if they had the time or the inclination, it would take many reporters to do it, and many more than we have.

Members of The Washington *Post* staff studied and analyzed the District courts for one year. In 1963, they found that twelve hundred and thirty-one felony indictments were returned against a total of fifteen hundred and nine defendants. Only three hundred and twelve of these cases, about one in every five, were ever mentioned at all, at any time, and to any extent in The Washington *Post*. This study shows that eighty percent of the persons committing major crime were never mentioned in print. The New York *Times* has pointed out that of the eleven thousand, seven hundred and twenty-four felonies committed in New York City in January, 1965, only forty-one were mentioned in the New York newspaper which gives most attention to crime — the New York *Daily News*.

The situation in the General Sessions Court of the District of Columbia is an example of the incredible volume of litigation that is being handled in our great cities. This court of fifteen judges deals each year with eighty-five thousand misdemeanor cases. (It handles, besides, a hundred thousand damage, small claims, and landlord and tenant suits.) Nearly a quarter of a million cases proceed each year through a court so crowded that it more resembles a city market than a court as clients and lawyers bicker and bargain and shop for judges.

The Washington *Post* took a close look at this court and obtained an astounding picture of its operations, which shocked and aroused the community and Congress, although it did not shock Congress sufficiently to induce it to provide an increase in the number of judges—not changed since 1950[8]—despite the fact that the case load has been increased seventy percent. More than a thousand criminal cases are awaiting trial. The average criminal case is tried three to six months after arrest. The civil case backlog includes five thousand civil damage suits (delay in handling them will average six months). There are more than three thousand domestic relations cases awaiting trial. The nation has a belief in jury trial—but in this court only ten in every hundred defendants ever ask for a jury trial and only one out of every ten ever finally reaches a jury.

The recent close scrutiny of this court is a credit to The Washington *Post* staff—but it cannot be claimed that the General Sessions Court, over the years, has had the kind of attention that would have kept this court, while trying, under trial. The City Desk of The Washington *Post* is just not staffed to give this lower court the kind of continuous scrutiny that would be equivalent to the public attention which Bentham, Wigmore, Blackstone, Cooley, and Acton were contemplating when they spoke of open courts and the benefits of publicity. The fact that the press *may* on occasion report what the judges say has some

[8] The number was increased by five in the last session.

restraining effect, but the fact that they seldom do report what the judges say and do, in the vast majority of cases, considerably diminishes any consolation to be derived from this solitary fact.

I have not had the opportunity to scrutinize the court coverage of other large cities to the extent necessary to support a flat assertion of inadequacy; but from what I have been able to learn by less than adequate resources of research, I feel that I will not be challenged by many newspapers if I say that the job we do by no means justifies the faith of the law writers in the beneficent effects of publicity upon the administration of justice.

And yet, I am aware that as I speak, in spite of an inadequacy in the press coverage of the courts, there is a cry rising from many sections of the public, and supported by much of the bar, that there is too much crime news in the press.

Now I know that this conviction in the bar springs from the anxiety that there is a conflict between "fair trial and free press." There is a long standing apprehension about this on the part of the bar. It became very vocal at the time of the Hauptman trial at Flemington, New Jersey, thirty years ago. It was aroused by the Halls-Mills case, the Sheppard case, the Rossinger case in California, and the Gosser case in Toledo—cases in which the press sensationalized the coverage and in some of which the newspapers sought to influence verdicts.

All of the earlier apprehensions were revived by newspaper handling of the assassination of President Kennedy, by coverage of the arrest and detention and murder of Oswald, and by the reporting of the Ruby trial. Lawyers voiced the conjecture that if Oswald had lived he could not have obtained a fair trial as a result of the publicity given the crime, the story of his arrest, the accounts of his detention, the news handling of the evidence against him. The President's Commission on the Assassination of President Kennedy blamed the press for a "part of the responsibility for the unfortunate circumstances following the President's death" and thought press and bar ought to join together to establish ethical standards on the dissemination of crime news "so that there will be no interference with pending criminal investigations, court proceedings, or the right of individuals to a fair trial."

It is interesting that the Commission did not suggest a legal remedy. No doubt they knew how difficult it would be to devise explicit rules. And the same difficulty has dogged the subsequent efforts of newspapermen and lawyers to set ethical standards of an extralegal sort. Some codes have been agreed to, here and there. But earnest lawyers and editors have found it beyond their ingenuity to set bounds upon the performance of the press that do not involve dangers to the contributions that the press legitimately makes to the administration of justice. When one considers the climate in which the Commission worked in the months following the President's assassination, it is not remarkable that the Commission's report reflected the anxiety of the commissioners. But in circumstances of this sort — where the life of the head of a nation is involved — new considerations are thrust into the case, considerations that, at the time, seem to the country and to the world, more important than the strict requirements of justice for the accused. Perhaps it is to acknowledge an indefensible fraility of our institutions to admit this, but I doubt if there is a remedy for this weakness if it is a weakness.

Let us assume that the first reaction of every law enforcement official in Texas to the President's assassination had been a determination so to conduct the detection and arrest and detention of the wrongdoer as to produce in court an accused person who could be brought before a jury with the presumption of innocence intact. The public officials, so motivated, let us assume, had suppressed all information about the location from which the assassination weapon was fired, concealed any references to the movement of the accused after the fatal act, disclosed no more than Oswald's name (and doubtfully that), divulged nothing of his identity or past record, gave out nothing about the origin of the weapon — or the number of shots — or whether one or more persons were suspect.

It is not difficult to imagine the consequences of that policy. The instant national reaction to the crime was that the President was the victim of a right-wing plot — and the secrecy which the best legal policy would have recommended might easily have fanned that suspicion into alarm, hate, and reprisal. As swiftly as this suspicion arose and declined, there was a nationwide suspicion that it was a Communist plot that felled the chief of state — and that suspicion and alarm, had it not been arrested by substantially accurate accounts in the press, might have produced untold reactions and unlimited reprisals. It offends our sense of justice to have to admit that any national consideration ever rises above the right of an individual accused person to a fair trial, but in every case of crime against the head of state in this country, public authority has been unwilling and unable to withhold information essential to quiet national alarm — even though disclosure prejudiced the full rights of the accused to appear before a jury and judge with the benefit of the presumption of innocence until proven guilty. We have not been willing to take steps — by statute or by policy — that would safeguard our system against this hazard. We have had to concede in fact — while we have been unwilling to admit in theory — that an individual in cases of this kind may not be able to get a fair trial within the ordinary meaning of that term. And I doubt that we can devise a system that will preclude this weakness. I even more gravely doubt that we ought to try to remodel our whole practice and policy, at the risk of depriving citizens of the security of open arrest and public trial, in order to make certain that in those fortunately rare instances where officials are the victims of crime the accused enjoy the perfect protection of the law.

The trial of Jack Ruby is another matter. The accused person who has killed a man in the presence of hundreds of witnesses, and whose act has been viewed on television by millions of persons, confronts the legal system with a very difficult proposition. I am not sure that any legal system, in such circumstances, could produce a jury satisfying all the requirements of impartiality or could assure the accused the full protection of the law. I am not saying that a miscarriage of justice resulted. I do not know that. I do admit that the coverage of the trial was not restrained. The television coverage was a caricature of the proper employment of this medium. It probably has fastened into the custom of most courts a ban on television for another generation. The Ruby trial proved that improvised television, utilizing old-fashioned equipment, not controlled by the court, is intrusive, obstructive, and disconcerting. But I trust proof of that did not await the Ruby trial. Courts should no more allow primitive cameras in a courtroom than they would allow newsmen to bring their presses into the chamber. But the Ruby case proved nothing, one way or another, about the feasibility or desirability of using modern unobtrusive equipment to widen the courtroom audience beyond the capacity of a courtroom. The effect of a proper camera on judge, lawyer, and witnesses is yet to be determined.

I have been dealing with spectacular crimes and events which I feel are beyond the reach of any remedy anyone has suggested. But, in fairness, there remains the question of less spectacular criminal cases. Are accused persons being deprived of fair trail by reason of newspaper publicity at the time of arrest, during pretrial examination, prior to trial, or at trial? How serious a problem is it?

In 1964 Attorney General Nicholas deB. Katzenbach said that twelve and a half percent of the cases involving Federal defendants went to trial and only eight percent were tried by juries. So we deal, at the outside, with eight percent of the Federal cases.

Judge Skelly Wright, of the D.C. Court of Appeals, has stated in discussing the issues of free press and fair trial that there is no problem at all in the great majority of the hundreds of thousands of criminal cases which are brought each year in this country because less than one percent of the cases are ever given a line of notice in the press and of that one percent seventy-five to ninety percent plead guilty. So, as Judge Wright has pointed out, what is involved is a small fraction of the less than one percent of the criminal cases brought.

The most thorough attempt on the part of the press to assess the frequency of the problem was made by Richard Cardwell, counsel for the Hoosier State Press Association. In the ten years between February, 1955, and February, 1965, he found seventy-four cases in which the issue of pretrial publicity was dealt with on appeal. In only seven cases did a reversal result. In the thirteen-year period prior to February, 1965, the issue of prejudicial publication during trial was raised on appeal in thirty-three cases and in only four cases did reversals result.

The District of Columbia study I referred to earlier showed that of all felony cases in 1963, only two percent received newspaper attention in circumstances where any prejudicial publication could have occurred. There is no evidence that any prejudicial publication did occur. There was not much risk of "trial by newspaper" in the General Sessions Court either. Only ten percent of the accused persons asked for a jury trial. Only ten percent of that ten percent got a jury trial. If every jury case had been prejudiced by publication, one percent of the cases would have been affected — and, of course, there is no allegation that this happened at all.

Still, the lawyers are right to worry if there is a single case in which the rights of the accused are prejudiced by publication — at arrest, in pretrial period, or at trial. If there should be a single miscarriage of justice — one that could have been prevented without adverse effect — it ought to be prevented. But if the prevention of rare injustices due to the publication can be achieved only by producing a great number of injustices arising from the more secret operation of the police and the courts, a different complexion is put upon the matter.

The number of cases is some measure of how much the problem ought to worry the bar and the press. And it is, moreover, an indication of whether we are justified in worrying about this defect more than we worry about some other remedial defects of our

J. R. WIGGINS

system of criminal justice. It seems to me that any rational examination of our courts will disclose larger worries. The number of defendants who are deprived of a fair trial by reason of their inability to obtain counsel must outnumber by a thousand to one the number who are denied a fair trial by reason of prejudicial publication. That this deprivation is indeed denial of a fair trial is being increasingly recognized by the courts, and it seems likely that within a generation the provision of counsel will be accepted as an obligation of the State that goes without saying.

The number of accused persons whose right to a fair trial is prejudiced by police disregard of the rights safeguarded under the Mallory rule limiting police power to detain and question prior to arraignment must exceed by a ratio of tens of thousands to one the number of persons at all adversely affected by pretrial publicity. And it needs to be said here, parenthetically, that one of the most powerful restraints upon the further denial of the rights of accused persons at the time of arrest and during prearraignment detention is the press — and the publicity the press is prepared to give to improper detention and questioning.

The number of accused persons who under our primitive bonding system suffer serious deprivation of rights by reason of inability to obtain bail and thereby suffer inability to achieve the freedom needed to perfect their own defense must be even greater. To be fair, many lawyers are worrying about this and are working to encourage the release of prisoners on their own recognizance.

The number of prisoners denied constitutional right to a speedy trial is steadily increasing as a result of the incredible congestion of our lower courts, and as a "fair trial" problem, they present a situation far more critical than any that arises because of publication.

Assistant Attorney General Ramsay Clark has recently said that eighty percent of the major crimes of violence in the United States are committed by youths who have previously been convicted of an earlier offense on a misdemeanor count. The whole theory that our system of arrest, trial, and punishment deters crime is called into doubt by such a figure. We have been brought to greater wisdom in the treatment of alcoholic offenders by recent decisions of the courts—decisions which may have the effect of relieving lower courts of a staggering percentage of their burdens. But we have gone on year after year, arresting, trying, and confining men and women for a disease, a process that surely will come to be regarded ultimately as something out of the

Dark Ages. Jail sentences have not deterred recidivism in alcoholics. Now that we have recognized that, can we ever be absolutely sure that mere imprisonment without treatment can cure shoplifting any more than it cures alcoholism? And is there any real hope that it can cure any other criminal impulse?

Our great penal institutions of maximum security are bulging with prisoners three fourths of whom will leave them to return to crime. There probably is no serious student of crime in this country who does not believe that a system of field supervision under conditions of minimal security would have a better chance of diminishing crime than does our system of maximum security. We are two centuries behind our scientific knowledge in the administration of our penal institutions. Our system is not restoring convicted persons to a place in our society; instead, it is confirming them in the tendencies and weaknesses which brought them into collision with the law. The larger use of a constructive system of supervision might, in the opinion of competent people in our own Department of Justice, cut recidivism fifty percent.

It is a tribute to the conscience of the bar that it worries about even a few cases in which justice may have been denied through pretrial publicity. It ought to worry about them. But it ought to worry much more about the administration of a system of retributive justice that neither corrects the criminal nor protects the public, that burdens the courts with hundreds of thousands of criminal cases the disposition of which does not solve past crimes or prevent future ones.

The newspapers ought to worry about the cases they prejudice by publicity. But they ought to worry a great deal more about their failure to convey to the American public a picture of criminal justice in this country, a picture sufficiently complete and sufficiently accurate to persuade the people and the Congress to bring our police, our courts, and our penal institutions into the twentieth century.[9]

[9] Since this paper was written the Reardon Committee of the American Bar Association has issued its report, *Fair Trial and Free Press.*
The recommendations of this committee, if carried into effect, would diminish public scrutiny of the law enforcement process. As James Bryce pointed out in 1893: "Democratic theory, which has done a mischief in introducing the elective system (for judges) partly cures it by the light of publicity which makes honesty the safest policy." If this light of publicity is shielded and obstructed enough fully to protect the accused it will be darkened enough fully to protect corruption, malpractice, and fraud in the law-endorcement process.